Arduino with Geike

Learn Arduino in 10 easy exercises...

YvesHanoulle and Geike Hanoulle

Arduino with Geike

Learn Arduino in 10 easy exercises...

YvesHanoulle and Geike Hanoulle

ISBN 9789082826296

Leanpub

This is a Leanpub book. Leanpub empowers authors and publishers with the Lean Publishing process. Lean Publishing is the act of publishing an in-progress ebook using lightweight tools and many iterations to get reader feedback, pivot until you have the right book and build traction once you do.

Tweet This Book!

Please help YvesHanoulle and Geike Hanoulle by spreading the word about this book on Twitter!

The suggested tweet for this book is:

I bought Geike's Arduino workshop manual on @leanpub https://leanpub.com/ArduinoWithGeike/ #ArduinoWorkshop

The suggested hashtag for this book is #ArduinoWorkshop.

Find out what other people are saying about the book by clicking on this link to search for this hashtag on Twitter:

#ArduinoWorkshop

Also By These Authors
Books by YvesHanoulle

Who is agile? Volume 1

Arduino met Geike

Who is agile in Nigeria?

The Leadership Game

CoachRetreat

Who is agile in South Africa?

Our house in the garden

Who is agile in Australia & New Zealand?

Programmeren voor kinderen

Create your own manifesto

PO as a service workshop

Who is agile in Ukraine?

Who is agile in India

Tips From The agile Trenches

Das Leadership-Spiel

The Scaling Ball Game

Pair Programming

Community TIPS for hiring great people

Who is agile in Singapore?

Gereedschapskist voor de Agile Coach –
Visualisatievoorbeelden

Books by Geike Hanoulle

Arduino met Geike

Contents

Recommendations

Very nice book actually, especially the texts in between are great (programming is searching for errors :)). I have laughed many times while reading, so great :) With the extensions, I also find it fun and educational. Especially that you refer to the internet to get something resolved. The learning experience is really ok!

Nele Van Beveren

I saw Geike at CoderDojo4Divas last year and was very impressed! The comprehensive manual provided the ideal guideline for all participants to get to know Arduino in a step-by-step manner. Together with Geike's enthusiasm and helpfulness, this became a top workshop!

Roos Dumont

You are cool
Jade (participant Geike's workshop Maker Faire 2019)

My first experience with Arduino was very nice and easy with your book. Well done.

Wout Uyttebroek (participant Geike's workshop Maker Faire 2019)

Great job, I enjoyed it!
Lena (participant Geike's workshop Maker Faire 2019)

Foreword

Hi,

In this mini-book we will use a series of exercises to discover a few possibilities of Arduino.

At the back of this manual, more difficult words are explained in a glossary. If you have never worked with Arduino, I recommend that you read this list before you begin the exercises. (It is of course your choice how you want to learn.)

Programming mainly means looking for errors. Especially to help you with this, we have a chapter with tips for finding errors.

This workshop consists of 10 exercises. Every exercise has the same format:

- Assignment
- Material
- Connecting
- Code
- Possible mistakes
- Expansion

For the expansion, the idea is to do them without looking at the solution.
If you do a workshop with me, you will only receive the solution for the expansions at the end of the workshop. These solution are in the book, my intention is that participants of

the workshop can solve these parts themselves. This way they are better prepared for the rest of the exercises. If you read this book on your own, when you make the exercises in this book, I hope you will not look at the solution of the extensions, I'm convinced that that way, you learn faster.

To help you during the exercises, it is best to save your code a lot.
What I always do, is make a copy of the code at the start of an exercise (or extension).
In other words save as exercise1.ino and extension1.ino. And while I am busy with the exercise, save regularly and save with that name again at the end of the exercise. (You can also use exercise1_Begin.ino and exercise1_End.ino)

When I do that, I can always return to the code of that exercise.
Real programmers use a source control system (like github) for that, my way, is our poor person source control system.

Asking Questions

Programming is not easy. Even the smartest developers are regularly stuck. They are asking for help to other programmers, are programming with two (PairProgramming) or looking for help on the internet. So when you don't immediately know what to do, that does not mean you are stupid. It means you are learning. People that program are always learning. That's because developers are usually creating something that does not exist. That means that as a developer, you will think regularly: damned, I don't know (how to do this). The smartest programers ask a lot for help. Because they know, by asking for help, they learn something.

I hope you have as much fun with learning Arduino as I do.

Greetings

Geike Hanoulle

Setup

Before we can start with the exercises, we must setup our work environment.

If you are at a workshop like CoderDojo4Divas[1] en Maker Faire Gent[2] this was already done for you.

In this chapter, I explain how this was done, so you can do the same at home.

First connect the Arduino with you computer, using an USB cable.

USB Port

The twee ports in the yellow circle are USB ports. In this picture the lowest of the two post is also a different kind of port. The connection in the green rectangle is an HDMI port, you can use this to connect an external screen to your computer. (We don't need this now)

---

[1]http://www.coderdojo4divas.be/nl/
[2]https://www.makerfairegent.be/geikes-arduino-workshop-zo

Your Arduino get it's power through the USB cable, from the computer. When the Arduino get's power, there is a light that turns on. This light we call the power-LED, and is mostly green. The power-LED has to be lid all the time. When you turn on the Arduino, there is a second LED that may light up on the Arduino. (Usually orange). Maybe that will blink. That is the LED that is connected to pin 13. And you will control that LED with code. (yes you will be the boss deciding what the Arduino should do.)

Arduino IDE preferences

Adjust the Arduino IDE "preferences" as follows:

- click File> Preferences
- a selection window opens.
- Select Language (Editor language) =⇒ select your native language
- Set the font size editor to 16 or larger,
- check Display line numbers.
- confirm with OK
- Close the IDE (the Arduino program) again and open it again.

the PC-Arduino connection

Now tell the PC which Arduino is connected and which USB port:

- click Tools> Board: choose Arduino / Genuino Uno
- click Tools> Port> and click on the USB port that lights up (with mention of your Uno)

The speaker

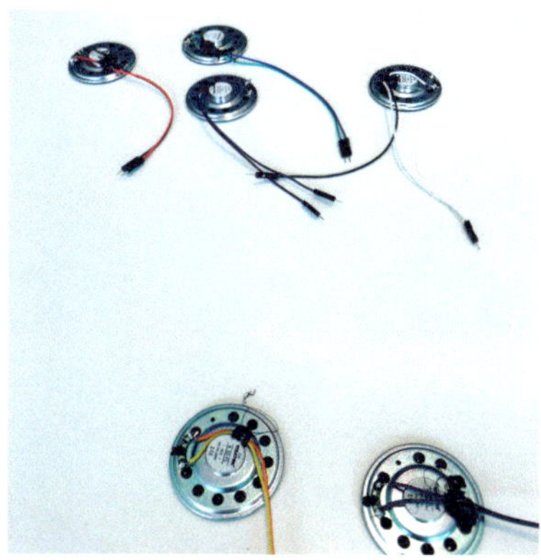

Speaker

The speaker that I bought can be used immediately, we don't need any resistor to connect it.

I did, however, solder a jumper wire to the speakers.

Because the jumper wire was very thin, I also glued the wire to the loudspeaker after soldering. This way, there was less chance that it got disconnected.

If the loudspeaker makes too much noise for you, you can always connect one of the loudspeaker wires via a resistor. The higher the resistance value, the less the current and … the quieter the speaker.

At the back of this manual you will find the material list that I use in this booklet. With also the necessary website addresses to purchase them.

The current website is a Belgium one.

Exercise one: let a LED on the Arduino light up

Assignment:

In the first assignment, we are going to let the LED on the Arduino light up.

- 1 second on (An Arduino thinks in milliseconden, so that is 1.000 milliseconds.)
- 1.000 milliseconds off.

Material:

- computer
- Arduino
- USB cable

Connecting:

In this first exercise we just have to connect the Arduino to the computer. We do this with the USB cable.

USB Port in the yellow circle

Code:

If you open the Arduino IDE, then you see this "empty" script.
(The program with code in Arduino is called a sketch.)

Empty Sketch

```
1  void setup() {
2    // put your setup code here, to run once:
3  }
4
5  void loop() {
6    // put your main code here, to run repeatedly:
7  }
```

If you don't see this, you go to the menu File and select the
option New.

In the empty sketch, you see two lines, that start with //
In the programming language for Arduino, we use // to say
that the rest of the line is a comment.

In other words, what follows the // is not used and is thus not converted in code that the Arduino understands. Yet only for that one line.

Comments

```
1   // We write comments to explain,
2   // explain what we do in the following code.
3   // Writing good comments is hard.
4   // Good comments explain:
5   //     * what we want to do
6   //     * why we want to do it
7   //     * NOT how we do it (for that we have
8   //     the code itself
9   // If you write good comments,
10  // it will help you when you later
11  // try to read your code.
12
13  void setup() {
14    // Here comes the code that is executed
15    // when the Arduino starts
16  }
17
18  // The function loop means that
19  // the code inside will be repeated.
20  void loop() {
21    // Here we add the code of our program,
22    // that will be repeated all the time.
23
24  }
```

To make the internal LED light up, we need to do three things.

- We define two variables: one for the pin number and one for the number of milliseconds.

The internal LED is connected with pin 13.

- We have to tell this pin to send power (to the LED), so it has to become an output pin.

(At the start up of the Arduino all pins are set as input pin, and can't send out power).

- we set the pin to HIGH, wait 1 second, and put the pin back to LOW

(If the pin is set to HIGH, power goes from the pin to the LED, and with that power the LED makes light.)

While you type this code, I advice you to check from time to time the code, with the option "check code"

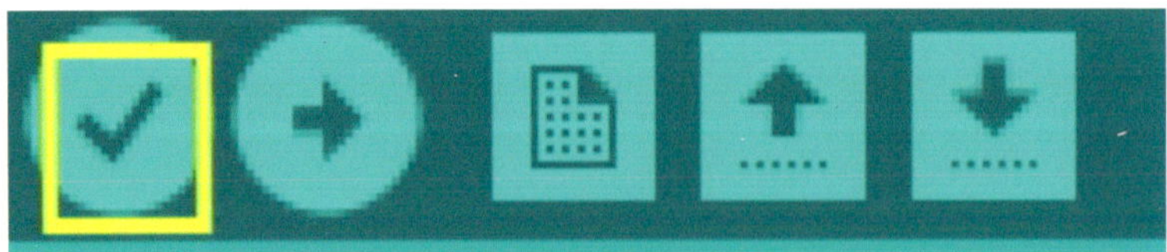

Check code

When you click on this check menu, your sketch is translated in ones and zeros (that is called compiling a program). Those ones and zero's are the only thing every computer understands. (And yes an Arduino might not be big, it's a computer. Did you know that this little Arduino is a more powerful computer than the one that was used to fly to the moon?). When this translation goes wrong, because of language mistakes in your sketch, you will get an error message, with an explanation that mentions a line number, in most cases the error is on this line or the line above.

```
expected ';' or ',' before 'void'                    Foutmeldingen kopiëren
exit status 1
expected ',' or ';' before 'void'
```

Error Message

Solution exercise one

```
1   const int ArduinoLightPin = 13;
2   const int TimeOn = 1000;
3   const int TimeOff = 1000;
4
5   void setup() {
6     // We set the pin to the OUTPUT position
7     pinMode(ArduinoLightPin, OUTPUT);
8   }
9
10  void loop() {
11    // We turn the light on
12    digitalWrite(ArduinoLightPin, HIGH);
13    // We wait a second
14    delay(TimeOn);
15    // We turn the light off
16    digitalWrite(ArduinoLightPin, LOW);
```

```
17    // We wait a second
18    delay(TimeOff);
19  }
```

After you wrote the code, you need to install it to your Arduino.
You can do this from the menu Sketch and then the option Upload.

Or using the arrow in the visual taskbar. In this screenshot, you can see that in the yellow square.

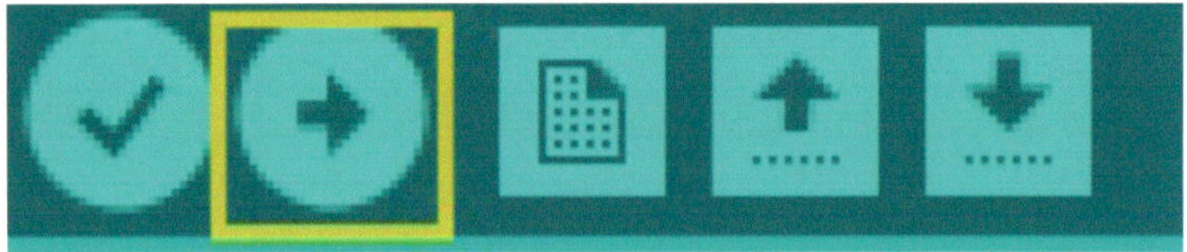

Upload arrow

When you click on this arrow, your sketch is translated and then send to the Arduino.
That is, it's send to your Arduino if the translated works. Otherwise, you will see the same error as when you click the check button.

Once it's send to your Arduino, it's stored in your Arduino and the Arduino immediately starts to execute your code.

Because sketch is stored in the Arduino, it will also be executed, if the Arduino is no longer connected to your computer, f ex when a battery nurtures the Arduino.
Without such nutrition the Arduino can't work. (I can't either, what about you?)

Some explanation:

- A line of code in Arduino we end with ;

Every programming language has it's own syntax. Just like French, Dutch, or English have their own spelling rules. The Arduino language expect you to finish a line of code with a ; . When you forget that, the compiler will only see that on the next instruction. Remember I told you that when you checked code, he might tell you the error is on the next line. The moment you forget a ; the error line will be on the next line for this reason.
It's a little bit like that annoying teacher that asks you: "Are you sure you did review your text?" You know she saw an error, yet she does not want to tell you were. Very annoying.

- int ArduinoLightPin = 13;

We use "int" to declare an integer (Aka a variable of type number). This means we make room available in the memory of the Arduino for a number without decimal. To find that number back, the variable "ArduinoLightPin" points to this memory. With the "=" sign we put the value 13 on that location of the memory. With this line of code we tell Arduino that the variable "ArduinoLightPin" has the value 13.
We use a variable, because in code "ArduinoLightPin" is more clear than "13".
And pin 13 is on most Arduino the PIN, that is connected to the LED on the bord. We can turn on this LED by put the value for pin 13 to HIGH.

- const

There are two kind of variables in a program.
Variables that can change, we define by writing INT.
There are also variables that are not allowed to change in the program.
In this case, the pin that wil need to get the power, will always be the same. Because you Arduino board won't change while the program is running. Even in the next exercises where we use a PIN that is connected with an external LED? The connection won't change while the program is running. We call these kind of variables constants.
In Arduino we use the word CONST to describe them. We put that word in front of the "int". (See the solution of exercise one. The first three lines are a few examples of this.

- pinMode(ArduinoLightPin, OUTPUT);

Here, we tell that the pin with number ArduinoLightPin (remember, that is 13), is an output pin.
Words in capitals, are also constants, and these constants have a fixed meaning in Arduino. And usually that meaning is defined by the people who created the Arduino language.)

- digitalWrite(ArduinoLightPin, HIGH);

We write to the pin with number ArduinoLightPin (aka 13) the value "HIGH".
This means, that the LED may turn on.

- delay(TimeOn);

We wait as long as TimeOn. We has TimeOn set to 1.000
That ment 1000 milliseconds, so we wait one second.

- void

This is a word, we use to tell that a function does not
return a value.
The are also function that do return a value, there void
will be replaced by the type of value the function returns.
(f ex int) We are not going to use these kind of functions
in this workshop.

- loop()

From the moment the function "setup" is finished, the
functie "loop" starts. And this function, repeats itself.

Possible mistakes:

- The definition of the variables are in the setup function,
  instead of before the setup.
- You forgot to add an ; at the end of a line. (Don't feel
  bad if you do, this is the most common mistake new
  programmers make.)
- capital and small letters are important. If you create a
  variable with capitals, you will need to use the exact
  writing in the program.

To make it yourself easy to spot the capital mistakes; it's best to have a one way to use capitals and small letters, in your whole program.
IN this book, we use one Capital for the first letter of a word, when used as a variable.

Like with TimeOn or ArduinoLightPin,

Extension:

What should you change so that the LED light stays on double long as it stays off?

The solution for the extension can be found at the end of the book.

Exercise two: let an external LED light up

Assignment:

In this challenge, the goal is to let an external LED light blink.

- One second the green LED is turned on.
- One second the green LED is turned off.

Material:

I only mention the new material you need.
So it's literally the material of last exercise + this list, that you need for this exercise.

- Breadboard
- Green LED light (Yes it is temping to use another color, yet that will make it harder to follow my instructions of future exercises.
- green jump wire (Yes you can use another color, if you follow our colourscheme, you can just copy our connection drawings.)
- black jump wire
- resistor 220 Ohm (colour of rings red/red/brown/- of red/red/black/black/-)

Connecting:

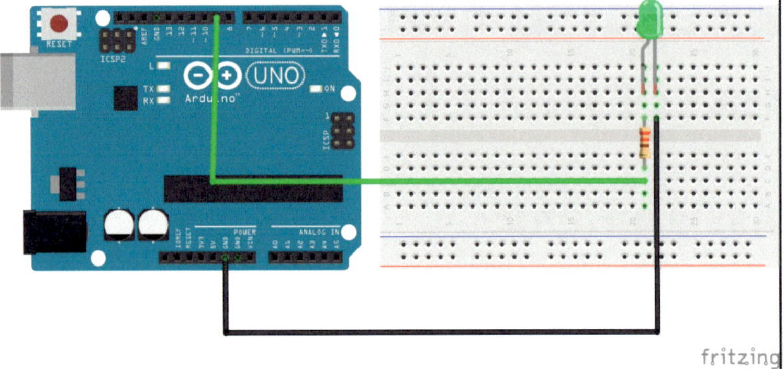

Connection exercise 2

As you can see on the drawing, we connect pin 9, using the resistor 220 OHM, with the long leg (Anode) of the green LED light.

Green LED light with longer leg.

We use a breadboard. A breadboard lets you connect wires, without the need to solder. On a breadboard the holes in the middle are connected in groups of five. The outside row of

holes, are connecting in two long rows. (blue & red)
If you put the connector a hole of a breadboard, you can connect it with the LED light, by putting one leg of the LED light in the same column of the breadboard.

After you connected the Arduino pin 9 connected with a resistor and the other side of the resistor to the long leg of the green LED, you have to connect the smallest leg of the LED with GND of the Arduino.
You can use any colour wire you want, I prefer to use a black jump wire for connections with GND. Having a colour standard, makes it easier to understand more complicated circuits.

Code:

Exercise two

```
1   const int GreenLedLightPin = 9;
2   const int TimeOn = 1000;
3   const int TimeOff = 1000;
4
5   void setup() {
6     // We set the pin to the output position
7     pinMode(GreenLedLightPin, OUTPUT);
8   }
9
10  void loop() {
11    // We turn the LED light on
12    digitalWrite(GreenLedLightPin,HIGH);
13    // We wait a second
14    delay(TimeOn);
15    // We turn the LED light off
```

```
16   digitalWrite(GreenLedLightPin, LOW);
17   // We wait a second
18   delay(TimeOff);
19 }
```

Possible mistakes:

- Be careful to use a resistor of 220 Ohm and not 220K Ohm, that last one will block too much power and your LED won't work.
- One mistake many people make is to connect the LED wrong. When it does not give any light, try turning the LED (aka swap the legs from place), with some LED's it's hard to see the difference between the long and the small leg.

Extension:

What should you change in your code, so you can connect the LED to PIN 8 ?

The solution for the extension two can be found at the end of the book.

Exercise three: swap between Arduino light and LED

Assignment:

In this challenge we swap between the Arduino light and the external LED light.

10.000 milliseconds we show the Arduino light.
1.000 milliseconds we turn on the green LED light.

Material:

No new material needed.

Connecting:

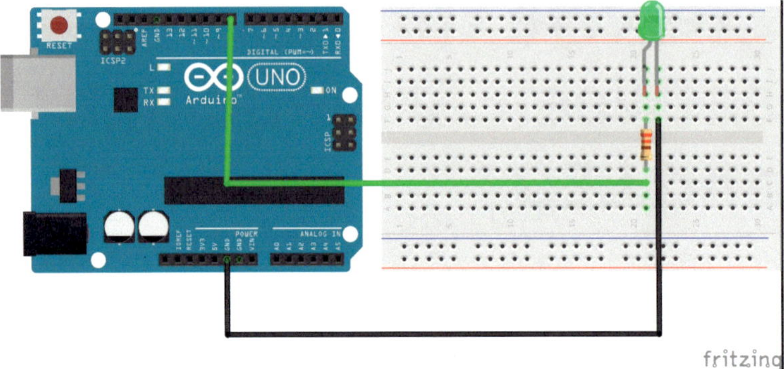

Connection excercise 3

This is the connection as we did it for the extension of exercise two.

Code:

Exercise three

```
1   const int ArduinoLightPin = 13;
2   const int GreenLedLightPin = 8;
3   const int TimeArduino = 10000;
4   const int TimeGreen = 1000;
5
6   void setup() {
7     // We set the pins to the output position
8     pinMode(GreenLedLightPin, OUTPUT);
9     pinMode(ArduinoLightPin, OUTPUT);
10  }
11
```

```
12  void loop() {
13    // We turn the Arduino light on and
14    // the green light off.
15    digitalWrite(ArduinoLightPin,HIGH);
16    digitalWrite(GreenLedLightPin, LOW);
17    // We wait ten seconds
18    delay(TimeArduino);
19    // We turn the Arduino light off and
20    // the green light on.
21    digitalWrite(ArduinoLightPin,LOW);
22    digitalWrite(GreenLedLightPin, HIGH);
23    // We wait a second
24    delay(TimeGreen);
25  }
```

Extension:

What should you adjust so that in between the two lights, you have a pauze of 2.000 milliseconds?

The solution for the extension three can be found at the end of the book..

Exercise four: red light

Assignment:

We start from the solution of extension three.
In this assignment we add a red LED light to pin 10.
We don't touch the connection of the green light. (We won't use it in the program)
We do this small little extra step, so that we know this connection works.
In the code we only change the pin number. We use pin 10 instead of pin 8.

Material:

The new necessities for the exercise four are:

- red LED lamp
- red jump wire
- two new black jump wire
- resistor 220 Ohm

Connecting:

Connection exercise 4

The outer two rows of holes, on the long sides of a breadboard, are connected to each other along the length of the board. This way we only have to connect one jumper to the GND. The agreement is that we use a blue hole row for GND. (And also a red hole row for the + 5V power supply). On the breadboard, we then connect the row of holes with both LEDs.

Code:

Exercise four

```cpp
//const int GreenLedLightPin = 8;
const int RedLedLightPin = 10;
const int ArduinoLightPin = 13;


const int TimeArduino = 10000;
//const int TimeGreen = 1000;
const int TimeRed = 1000;
const int TimeWait = 2000;

void setup() {
  // We set the pins to the output position
  pinMode(RedLedLightPin, OUTPUT);
  pinMode(ArduinoLightPin, OUTPUT);
}

void loop() {
  // We turn the Arduino light on and
  // the red light off.
  digitalWrite(ArduinoLightPin,HIGH);
  digitalWrite(RedLedLightPin, LOW);
  // We wait ten seconds
  delay(TimeArduino);

  // We turn both lights off
  digitalWrite(ArduinoLightPin,LOW);
  digitalWrite(RedLedLightPin, LOW);

  // We wait two seconds
  delay(TimeWait);

  // We turn the red light on
  digitalWrite(RedLedLightPin, HIGH);
```

```
33
34    // We wait a seconde
35      delay(TimeRed);
36    }
```

You can see that the variables for the green LED light are still in our code. I have commented those lines of code so that they do not work. I did not want to remove these lines because we will need them later. That was of course not mandatory. When you have remove these lines, it actually gives nicer code. (Never keep code in comments just in case, that is a bad habit.)

Extension:

In this expansion you must ensure that there is no longer any waiting time between the Arduino light and the red LED.

The solution for the extension four can be found at the end of the book..

Exercise five: red and green

Assignment:

In this assignment we alternate the green LED light with a red LED light.
A bit like a pedestrian light works at a traffic light. We therefore have to wait twice as long as we have time to cross. (Cars get more time to drive for some reason ...)

- 10 seconds we turn the green LED light on.
- 20 seconds we turn the red LED light on (and the green off).

Material:

No new material needed for exercise five.

Connecting:

The connections of exercise five and those of exercise four are the same. (If you did not remove the connections for the green LED)

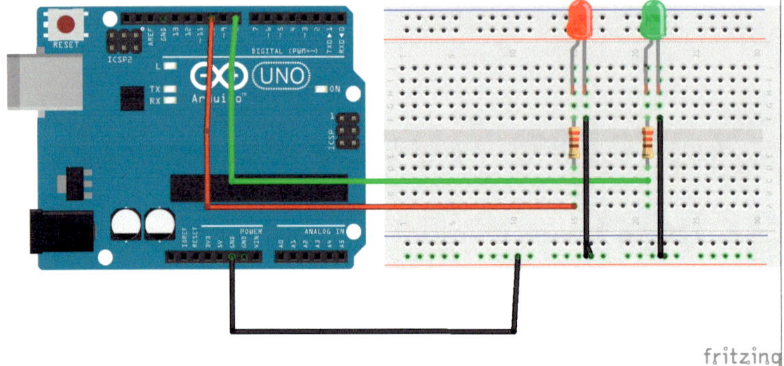

Connection exercise 4 & 5

Code:

Exercise Five

```
1  const int GreenLedLightPin = 8;
2  const int RedLedLightPin = 10;
3  //const int ArduinoLightPin = 13;
4
5  //const int TimeArduino = 10000;
6  const int TimeGreen = 10000;
7  const int TimeRed = 20000;
8
9  void setup() {
10   // We set the pins to the output position
11   pinMode(RedLedLightPin, OUTPUT);
12   pinMode(GreenLedLightPin, OUTPUT);
13 }
14
15 void loop() {
16   // We turn the green light on and
17   // the red light off.
```

```
18    digitalWrite(GreenLedLightPin,HIGH);
19    digitalWrite(RedLedLightPin, LOW);
20
21    // We wait ten seconds
22    delay(TimeGreen);
23
24    // We turn the green light off and
25    // the red light on.
26    digitalWrite(GreenLedLightPin,LOW);
27    digitalWrite(RedLedLightPin, HIGH);
28
29    // We wait twenty seconds
30    delay(TimeRed);
31  }
```

Extension:

What should you adjust so that the red light stays on for a random time?

Tip: search the internet for the combination of Arduino and random.
Search the internet for the combination of Arduino and random. Or use the reference work that was installed with the Arduino software. Go to the Help menu and then Reference work.

The Reference Work opens with a "glossary". You can click on each word for more explanation. What we are looking for is in the right-hand column at the bottom, under Random Numbers.
If it gives a problem on your computer, you can also find the

info on random online[3]

The solution for the extension five can be found at the end of
the book..

---

[3]https://www.arduino.cc/reference/en/language/functions/random-numbers/
random/

Exercise six: a yellow LED light

Assignment:

In this assignment we add a yellow LED. In this exercise we ignore the green light for a moment. And we ensure that the yellow LED light alternates with the red LED light.

As you probably understood by now, I try to limit the changes you need to make. This way, you can test our changes as quickly as possible. That is a great way to get faster feedback, something I find important when I program.

Material:

We need this extra material:

- yellow LED lamp
- yellow jumper wire
- black jumper wire
- resistor 220 Ohm

Connecting:

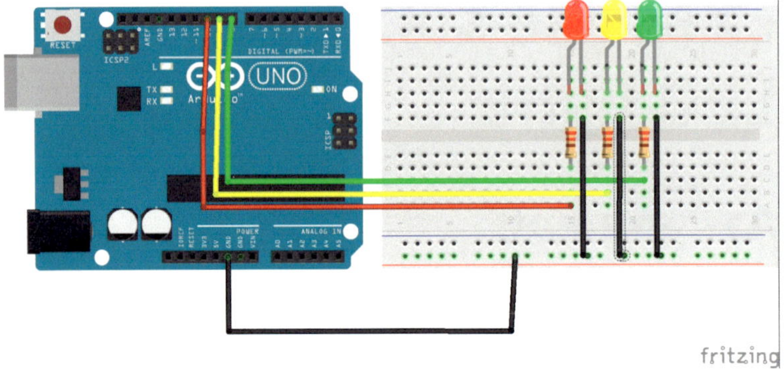

Connection exercise six

Code:

exercise six

```
1   const int GreenLedLightPin = 8;
2   const int YellowLedLightPin - 9;
3   const int RedLedLightPin = 10;
4
5   const int TimeGreen = 10000;
6   const int TimeYellow = 10000;
7   //const int TimeRed = 20000;
8
9   const int MinRandom=100;
10  const int MaxRandom=10000;
11  long RandomTime;
12
13  void setup() {
14    // We set the pins to the output position
```

```
15    pinMode(RedLedLightPin, OUTPUT);
16    pinMode(YellowLedLightPin, OUTPUT);
17    pinMode(GreenLedLightPin, OUTPUT);
18    randomSeed(analogRead(0));
19  }
20
21  void loop() {
22    // We turn the yellow light on and
23    // the red light off.
24    digitalWrite(YellowLedLightPin,HIGH);
25    digitalWrite(RedLedLightPin, LOW);
26
27   // We wait ten seconds
28    delay(TimeYellow);
29
30    // We turn the yellow light off and
31    // the red light on.
32    digitalWrite(YellowLedLightPin,LOW);
33    digitalWrite(RedLedLightPin, HIGH);
34
35    // We calculate the random time for
36    // the red light.
37    // This time is between MinRandom and MaxRandom.
38    // It's as if it stays red, till a car arrives
39    RandomTime = random( MinRandom, MaxRandom);
40    delay(RandomTime);
41  }
```

Extension:

In this extension you need to remove the random functionality out the exercise.

The solution for the extension six can be found at the end of the book..

Exercise seven: a traffic light

Assignment:

In this assignment we alternate red, yellow and green.

20 seconds on green
5 seconds on yellow
20 seconds on red

Material:

No new material needed.

Connecting:

Same connection exercise six.

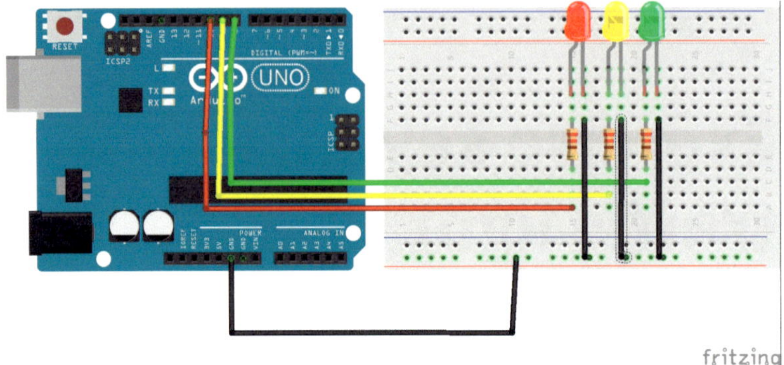

Connection exercise 6 & 7

Code:

Exercise seven

```
1   const int GreenLedLightPin = 8;
2   const int YellowLedLightPin = 9;
3   const int RedLedLightPin = 10;
4
5   const int TimeGreen = 20000;
6   const int TimeYellow = 5000;
7   const int TimeRed = 20000;
8
9   void setup() {
10    // We set the pins to the output position
11    pinMode(RedLedLightPin, OUTPUT);
12    pinMode(YellowLedLightPin, OUTPUT);
13    pinMode(GreenLedLightPin, OUTPUT);
14  }
15
16  void loop() {
17    // We turn the green light on and
```

```
18    // the yellow & red light off.
19    digitalWrite(GreenLedLightPin,HIGH);
20    digitalWrite(YellowLedLightPin, LOW);
21    digitalWrite(RedLedLightPin, LOW);
22
23    // We wait twenty seconds
24    delay(TimeGreen);
25
26     // We turn the yellow light on and
27    // the green & red light off.
28    digitalWrite(GreenLedLightPin, LOW);
29    digitalWrite(YellowLedLightPin, HIGH);
30    digitalWrite(RedLedLightPin, LOW);
31
32     // We wait five seconds
33    delay(TimeYellow);
34
35    // We turn the red light on and
36    // the yellow & green light off.
37    digitalWrite(GreenLedLightPin, LOW);
38    digitalWrite(YellowLedLightPin, LOW);
39    digitalWrite(RedLedLightPin, HIGH);
40
41     // We wait twenty seconds
42    delay(TimeRed);
43 }
```

Extension:

In this extension, the intention is to make the yellow light blink during the waiting time.

The solution for the extension seven can be found at the end of the book..

Exercise eight: button

Assignment:

In this assignment we add a push button.

Standard green light.
When the button is pressed, the yellow LED will flash.
Afterwards 10,000 milliseconds on red.

Then the green comes back on.

Material:

- button
- orange jumper wire
- blue jumper wire
- black jumper wire
- resistor 220 ohm

Connecting:

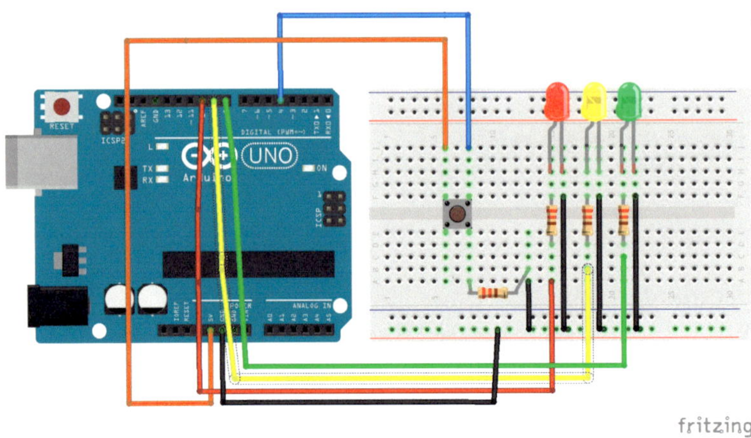

Connection exercise 8

Code:

exercise eight

```
1   const int ButtonPin = 4;
2
3   const int GreenLedLightPin = 8;
4   const int YellowLedLightPin = 9;
5   const int RedLedLightPin = 10;
6
7   const int TimeGreen = 20000;
8   const int TimeYellow = 1000;
9   const int TimeRed = 10000;
10
11  int ButtonStatus = 0;
12
13  void setup() {
```

```cpp
14    // We set the pins to the output position
15    pinMode(RedLedLightPin, OUTPUT);
16    pinMode(YellowLedLightPin, OUTPUT);
17    pinMode(GreenLedLightPin, OUTPUT);
18    pinMode(ButtonPin, INPUT);
19  }
20
21  void loop() {
22    // We turn the green light on and
23    // the yellow & red light off.
24    digitalWrite(GreenLedLightPin,HIGH);
25    digitalWrite(YellowLedLightPin, LOW);
26    digitalWrite(RedLedLightPin, LOW);
27
28    ButtonStatus = digitalRead(ButtonPin);
29
30    if (ButtonStatus == HIGH) {
31      // We turn the yellow light on and
32      // the green & red light off.
33      digitalWrite(GreenLedLightPin, LOW);
34      digitalWrite(YellowLedLightPin, HIGH);
35      digitalWrite(RedLedLightPin, LOW);
36
37      // blink
38      delay(TimeYellow);
39      digitalWrite(YellowLedLightPin, LOW);
40      delay(TimeYellow);
41      digitalWrite(YellowLedLightPin, HIGH);
42      delay(TimeYellow);
43      digitalWrite(YellowLedLightPin, LOW);
44      delay(TimeYellow);
45      digitalWrite(YellowLedLightPin, HIGH);
46      delay(TimeYellow);
```

```
47
48       // We turn the red light on and
49       // the yellow & green light off.
50       digitalWrite(GreenLedLightPin, LOW);
51       digitalWrite(YellowLedLightPin, LOW);
52       digitalWrite(RedLedLightPin, HIGH);
53
54       // We wait ten seconds
55     delay(TimeRed);
56   }
57 }
```

IF
In the code we have used **if**.
After an if there is a condition in parentheses.
A condition can be right or wrong. (For a computer **true** or **false**)
If the condition is correct, the code between the braces is executed.

There is also a **else** that is executed if the condition in the if is "wrong". (And as you can see in the underlying code, there is also a **else if**. I think you know what this means.)

if else

```
1   if (condition one)
2   {
3     // do code one
4   }
5   else if (condition two)
6   {
7     // do code two
8   }
9   else
10  {
11    // do code three
12  }
```

Possible mistakes:

- The orange jumper wire from the button must be connected with the Arduino with 5V, not with the GND.
- The button has four pins, they should be connected two by two parallel with the long sides of the breadboard. This is hard to explain, if you are not sure you understand, turn the button a quarter turn. (It does not matter if you turn left or right.)

Extension:

No extension for this exercise.

Exercise nine: sound

Assignment:

In this assignment we add a loudspeaker.
While the red light is on, a sound (440 hertz) will be heard.

Material:

We need a loudspeaker for this exercise.

- loudspeaker
- black jump wire
- white jump wire

Connecting:

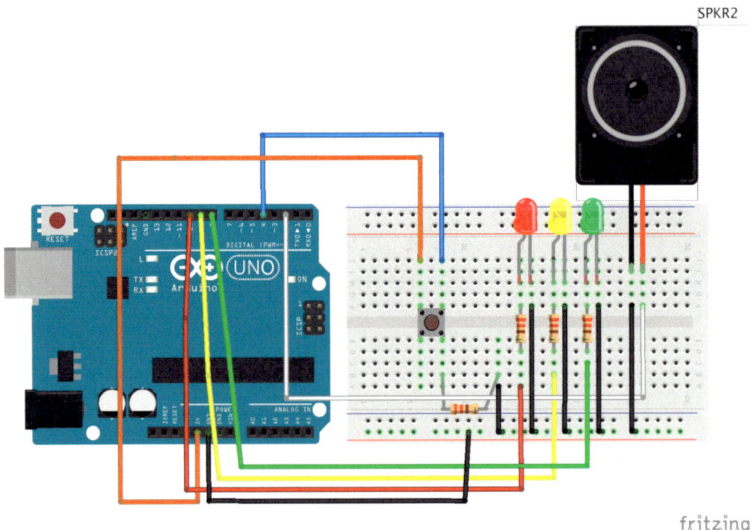

Connection exercise 9

Code:

exercise nine

```
1   const int SpeakerPin = 2;
2   const int ButtonPin = 4;
3   const int GreenLedLightPin = 8;
4   const int YellowLedLightPin = 9;
5   const int RedLedLightPin = 10;
6
7   const int TimeGreen = 20000;
8   const int TimeYellow = 1000;
9   const int TimeRed = 10000;
10
```

```
11  const int  StuttgartPitchFrequency  = 440;

12

13  int ButtonStatus = 0;

14

15  void setup() {

16

17   // We set the pins to the output position
18    pinMode(RedLedLightPin, OUTPUT);
19    pinMode(YellowLedLightPin, OUTPUT);
20    pinMode(GreenLedLightPin, OUTPUT);
21    pinMode(ButtonPin, INPUT);
22    pinMode(SpeakerPin, OUTPUT);
23  }

24

25  void loop() {
26    // We turn the green light on and
27    // the yellow & red light off.
28    digitalWrite(GreenLedLightPin,HIGH);
29    digitalWrite(YellowLedLightPin, LOW);
30    digitalWrite(RedLedLightPin, LOW);

31

32    ButtonStatus = digitalRead(ButtonPin);

33

34    if (ButtonStatus == HIGH) {

35

36            // We turn the green light on and
37            // the yellow & red light off.
38            digitalWrite(GreenLedLightPin,HIGH);
39            digitalWrite(YellowLedLightPin, LOW);
40            digitalWrite(RedLedLightPin, LOW);

41

42          // blink
43          delay(TimeYellow);
```

```cpp
        digitalWrite(YellowLedLightPin, LOW);
        delay(TimeYellow);
        digitalWrite(YellowLedLightPin, HIGH);
        delay(TimeYellow);
        digitalWrite(YellowLedLightPin, LOW);
        delay(TimeYellow);
        digitalWrite(YellowLedLightPin, HIGH);
        delay(TimeYellow);

        // We turn the red light on and
            // the yellow & green light off.
        digitalWrite(GreenLedLightPin, LOW);
        digitalWrite(YellowLedLightPin, LOW);
    digitalWrite(RedLedLightPin, HIGH);

        // This next function is split over two lines
        // for the book. You can write it on one
        // line.
        tone(SpeakerPin, StuttgartPitchFrequency,
            TimeRed);
        // We wait ten seconds
        delay(TimeRed);
    }
}
```

Extension:

With this expansion you have to alternate the sound between 960 hertz and 770 hertz. The period for a sound must be 1.3 seconds.

The solution for the extension nine can be found at the end of the book..

Exercise ten: pedestrian light

Assignment:

In this assignment we will add a pedestrian light next to the traffic light.
Think for a moment how a traffic light and a pedestrian light work together.
The pedestrian light consists of a red and green LED.

For this exercise, you have to figure everything out yourself.

Material:

For this larger exercise we immediately need a lot of extra material:

- green LED light
- green jumper wire
- two black jumper wires
- red LED light
- red jumper wire
- two resistors 220 ohms

Code:

No code from us, you have to figure this one out on your own.

Extension:

Since we do not provide a solution for this exercise, the entire exercise ten is the extension. You can find the connection in the expansion solution.

The solution for the extension ten can be found at the end of the book..

Glossary

- Arduino

An Arduino uno

An Arduino is a cheap mini computer. This platform is ment for hobbyists & artists.

- Arduino IDE

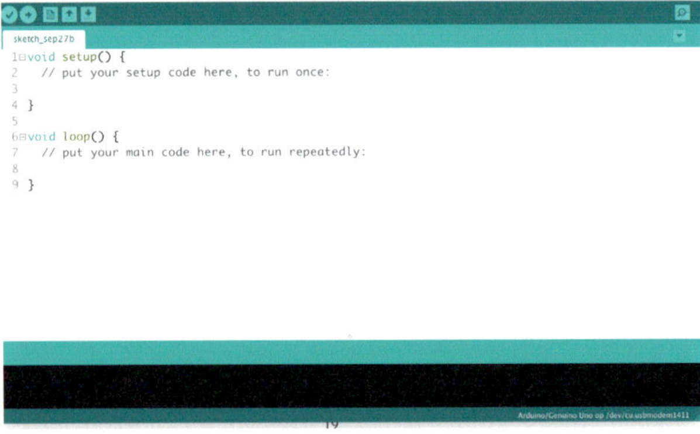

The Arduino IDE

The Arduino can be programmed with the Arduino IDE. This software makes it easy to write your own code and upload it to an Arduino. A program made in the Arduino IDE is called a "sketch" or sketch. The Arduino IDE is open source and can be downloaded for free from the Arduino site[4].

- Arduino pins.

---

[4]https://www.arduino.cc/

The pins on an Arduino

We have pins on an Arduino sign. We call it pins, but they are actually holes where you can insert a pin.
There are different types of pins.

- 14 digital pins in an Arduino. These are both input and output pins. (pins 0-13)
- 6 analog input pins (0-5)
- 6 analog output pins (3,5,6,9,10,11)

Although they are actually digital pins that you say through a program to behave analogously.

- Breadboard

A breadboard

A breadboard ensures that you can connect wires without having to solder them together. With a breadboard, the holes in the middle are connected to each other in five columns. The outer two long rows of holes are connected in two rows (blue and red).

If you insert the jig of a jumper wire into a hole in a breadboard, you can connect to the LED light by poking a leg of the LED into a hole in the same column.

- Jumperwire / Jump wire / Jumper

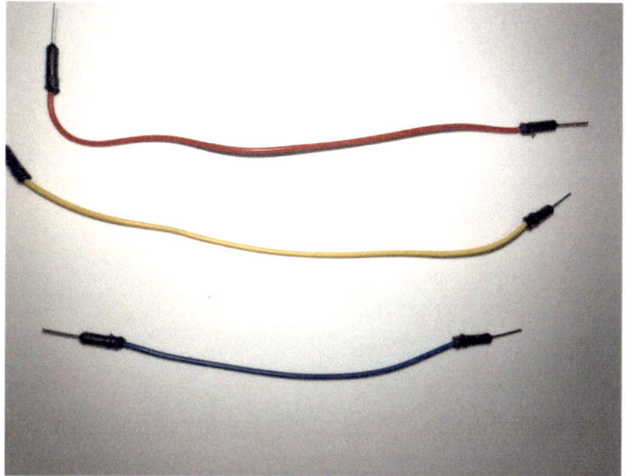

Jumperwires

There is no difference between the different colors of jumper wires. they only help to recognize. You may not have the same colors to make the connections. That's OK.

* LED

LED's

The LED lights have two different legs.
A long leg (+) also called anode and a short leg (-) also called

a cathode.

- Multimeter

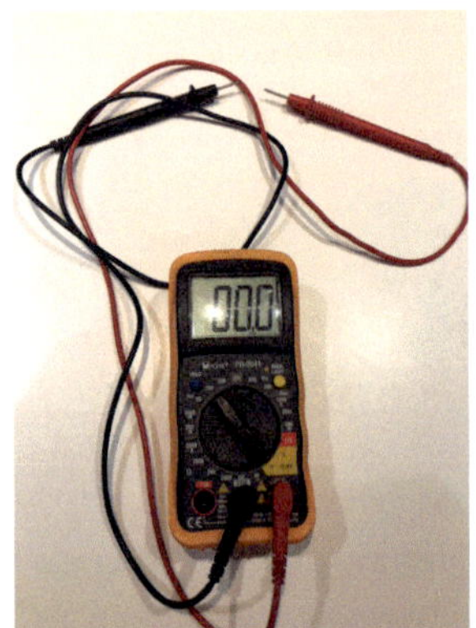

A multimeter

With a multimeter you can measure the electrical values such as voltage, current and resistance. How you can use that multimeter is explained in the paragraph multimeter.

- Milliseconds

A thousand milliseconds go in 1 second, just as 1000 millimeters go in 1 meter.
If you pass on time to the Arduino, you have to do that in milliseconds.

- Variable

A variable is a kind of box where we can insert a number, we can see what is in it, add it or take it out, and change the content. Variables get a place in the memory of the Arduino.

There are small and large boxes. The smallest one, a "byte", takes 8 bits. You can put 1 letter in it, or a number between 0 and 255. For larger numbers you need more bits: in an "int" (16 bit) a number can be between -32.768 and 32.767. You give each variable in your code a name (otherwise you won't find that "box"!). The name must begin with a letter. Choose the name well, so that you later know what you wanted to use the box for.

- Resistor

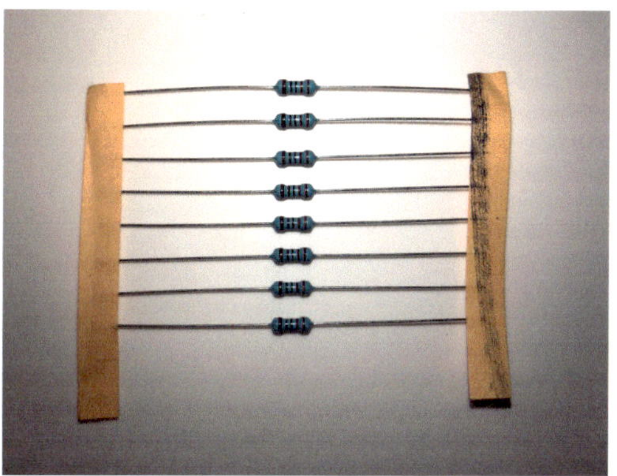

Resistors

Sometimes the electricity that an Arduino transmits is too powerful for certain components such as the LED lights. If that is the case, then we use a resistor to ensure that the current is obstructed. There are different types of resistors that allow more or less current to pass through.
How you can calculate that resistance is explained in the resistance section

Finding errors

Programming is primarily about making mistakes.

Write something that you are sure works.
Execute the code. It does not work
Change something. It does not work.
Change something else. It still doesn't work agghh !!!!
A long time later ...
Ah now it works. Why?

Finding errors

This chapter contains tips about what you can do wrong.

There are two types of programming errors.

Syntax errors

With syntax errors, the Arduino does not understand what you are saying. Syntax errors are spelling errors for the computer. A computer is a bit like a language teacher, if there is a spelling error, she will tilt and stops trying to understand what you wrote.

You can find syntax errors by verifying your program. You do that by pushing a button that looks like a check mark.

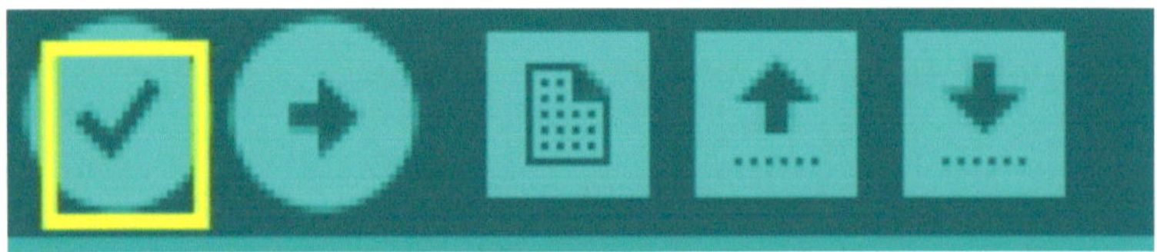

Verify

If there are syntax errors, you will receive an error message at the bottom.

```
expected ',' or ';' before 'void'                    Foutmeldingen kopiëren

exit status 1
expected ',' or ';' before 'void'
```

Error message

In the code you also see a line that is indicated.

```
2  int EenSeconde = 1000
3
4  void setup() {
5
```

Line four is marked in rose.

Take a good look at the error message. And now look at the code. Do you see the error?

The computer gives a strange message. He says he misses a ";" But that error is not on line four, but on line two.

The computer says that for the command "void", the previous line must be closed with a ";"

Logical errors

You also have logical errors. That is a mistake where you ask a computer something he understands, but where you should have asked him something else. For example, you ask him to add two numbers, but you should have multiplied them. The result is wrong, but the computer cannot know that.

Experienced developers also make mistakes

A list of possible syntax errors

- Forgetting to put a ; at the end of a line.
- the definition of the variables, are in the setup (error) instead of before (correct).
- Uppercase and lowercase letters are important. If you create a variable with capital letters, you must also use it in your program.

- Forgetting a brace: for every {, there must be a } in your program.
- For functions such as **if** we use { and } to indicate which piece of code may only be executed if the condition in the if is correct. If you do not use { }, only the next line will be executed under the conditions of the if. The following lines of code are then always executed.

Connection mistakes

With Arduino you also have a third kind of error: connection mistakes.

- a jumperwire is in the wrong connection pin on the Arduino.
- A jumperwire is in teh wrong row/column on the bread-board.
- You used the wrong resistor.

Resistors

Sometimes the electricity that an Arduino transmits is too powerful for certain parts such as the LED lights. If that is the case, then we use a resistor to ensure that the current is obstructed. There are different types of resistors that allow more or less current to pass through. A resistor always has a few coloured rings.

Together these rings represent the value of the resistance according to this table.

Color	1e	2e	3e	Multiplier	Tolerance
Black	0	0	0	1 OHM	
Brown	1	1	1	10 OHM	+/- 1%
Red	2	2	2	100 OHM	+/- 2%
Orange	3	3	3	1.000 OHM	
Orange	3	3	3	1 kOHM	
Yellow	4	4	4	10 kOHM	
Green	5	5	5	100 kOHM	+/- 0,5%
Blue	6	6	6	1 MOHM	+/- 0,25%
Purple	7	7	7	10 MOHM	+/- 0,1%
Gray	8	8	8	100 MOHM	+/- 0,05%
White	9	9	9	1 GOHM	
Gold				0,1 OHM	+/- 5%
Silver				0,01 OHM	+/- 10%

In this workshop we mainly use a 220 OHM. We try to recognize this as an exercise.

With a four-band:
ring 1: red $\Rightarrow$ 2

ring 2: red ⇒ 2
ring 3 not
Multiplier: brown ⇒ 10 OHM
Tolerance: yellow ⇒ +/- 5%
This gives 2 2 *10 OHM =⇒ 220 OHM with 5% tolerance

With a five-band:
ring 1: red ⇒ 2
ring 2: red ⇒ 2
ring 3: back ⇒ 0
Multiplier: zwart ⇒ 1 OHM
Tolerance: brown ⇒ +/- 2%
This gives 2 2 0 * 1 OHM =⇒ 220 OHM with 2% tolerance

A high resistance value means that the current is more difficult to pass through the resistor. At a fixed voltage, e.g. 5 volts from the Arduino, therefore runs less current due to a higher resistance.

Multimeter

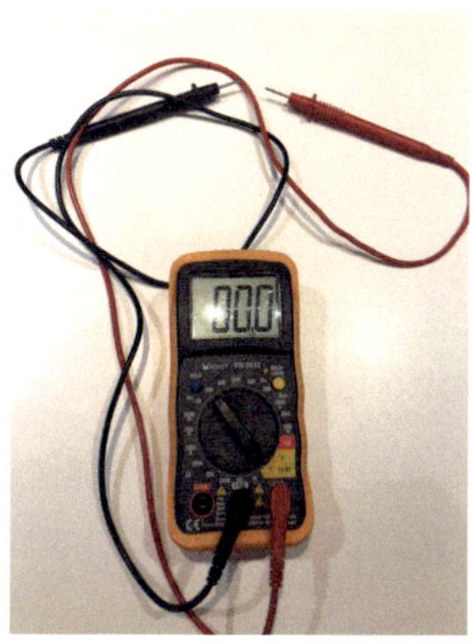

Multimeter

With a multimeter you can measure the electrical values such as voltage, current and resistance.

Measure	Value	Abbreviation
Spanning	Volt	V
Stroom	ampere	A
Weerstand	ohm	Ω

We will only measure resistances for the Arduino.
On the photo you see a digital multimeter.
You have the following positions on that.

Measuring range	Position
0 to 200 Ω	200
200 Ω to 2k Ω	2k
2k Ω to 20k Ω	20k
20k Ω to 200k Ω	200k
200k Ω to 2M Ω	2M

We use a 220 Ω resistor in the exercises.

The multimeter has two wires, one black and one red, with a measuring pin attached to it.
Connect the black wire with COM.
The red wire with the V / Ω (OHM) clamp.
Make sure the wires do not get mixed up.

Set the multimeter to the 2000 (2K) position.
As the table shows, we then measure values between 200 and 2000 ohms.
You can also measure smaller values, but less accurately, because you use fewer numbers on the display.
Is the value greater than 2K, e.g. because you have not yet connected a resistor, the display usually only shows a 1 on the far left.
To measure a resistor, you must connect each "leg" of the resistor to one of the test probes.
That can be "hands-free" with (crocodile) clips, but if you don't have one, you can do it like this:
Take a measuring pen in each hand, the pen on your index finger. And then clamp the resistance on the pins with your thumbs.
You clamp the red pin on one side of the resistor and the black pin on the other side.
The multimeter applies a low voltage to measure the resistance, but it is so low that you don't feel it.

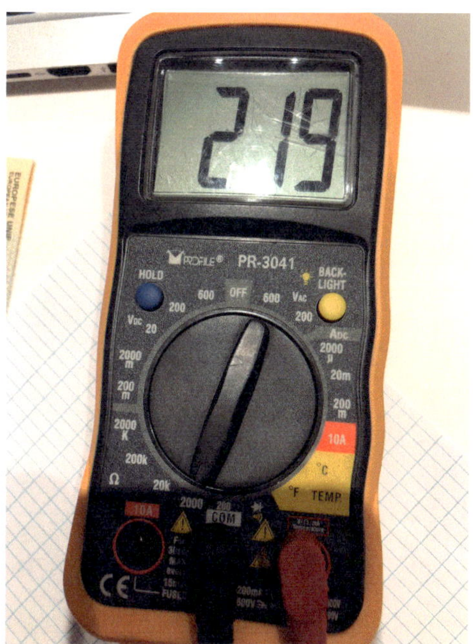

Result

If you have found the correct resistor (220 Ohm, marked with red red black black -) then the result will be a number that is close to the 220.

CoderDojo

At CoderDojo, girls and boys from 7 to 18 years old can learn to program. This is provided completely free of charge by volunteers!

Are you older? Then come help with a Dojo or start your own CoderDojo!

Mission

CoderDojo is a worldwide non-profit movement founded by James Whelton and Bill Liao.

The CoderDojo story started in early 2011 at James Whelton's school when he became familiar with hacking the iPod Nano. Some younger students asked him if he wanted to teach them how to program. James therefore established a computer club in his school, where he started teaching HTML and CSS basics. Later that year he met Bill Liao, an entrepreneur who wanted to make the project bigger. In June 2011 the first CoderDojo was launched in Cork. The event was a huge success and the popularity of CoderDojo grew rapidly. Shortly thereafter, the first Dojo in Dublin was born. By making the movement open source, CoderDojos were set up in no time throughout Ireland and later all over the world!

Next to normal CoderDojo's, CoderDojo organises also special events.

Coolest projects

CoderDojo is organizing "Coolest Projects" every year. Children and young people between 7 and 18 years old are given a stage to present their own technological design to the public. Moreover, these young inventors have the chance to win great prizes. The emphasis is not on winning but on participating. Every technological project is welcome. Machines that sort Lego bricks by color, funny games in Scratch, mouse traps that you text when you have caught a mouse,... Whoever participates is already cool anyway!

There is also a lot to experience at our fair for visitors. In addition to the projects of the participants, everyone can also enjoy themselves in our tech hang-out. Numerous fun gadgets such as 3D printers, a hololens, a real FabLab on wheels and a 'Pepper' robot provide extra entertainment.

Like all CoderDojo activities, Coolest Projects is completely free.
More info on: https://coolestprojects.org/

CoderDojo 4 Diva's

CoderDojo4Diva's is an annual event especially for girls in Belgium. We notice that the majority of our participants on regular Dojos are still boys. That is a shame, because everyone can program and girls are no exception.

That is why we organize a dojo especially for them and we unleash our creativity all day long on computer games, electronics and robots. Together with our junior coaches we show that programming is cool and that much more is possible than racing games and shooter games. Beginner or advanced; shy or exuberant; bookworm, sports fanatic or fashionista - there are no thresholds on CoderDojo4Divas!

More info you can find on: www.coderdojo4divas.be

CliniCoders

CliniCoders, is a project where children with long-term illnesses (in the hospital) get the chance to enjoy a few hours of programming pleasure. This project is already taking place in the hospitals of UZ Antwerpen, UZ Gent, AZ Groeninge and UZ Gasthuisberg.

During CliniCoders, the participating children are accompanied by children's coaches, who in turn are assisted by an adult lead coach. We do this to also promote social interaction between the participants and the child coaches.

Maker faire

A party!
An event!
A festival!

You can best describe a Maker Faire as a crazy do-it-yourself fair where everything is possible and allowed. Robotic arms, a fire-breathing dragon, a rope-jumping penguin, … You can't think of it strangely enough or you'll come across it.

In the first place it therefore becomes a showcase for creativity and ingenuity with the coolest projects and ideas of the moment. But workshops, keynote speeches and Maker Faire comedy nights will also be organized.

Material list

- Arduino uno
- breadboard
- jumperwire
- coloured LEDs
- loudspeaker

The material set we use is purchased from the web store Gotron[5].

We bought:

- Arduino UNO RV3 programming board: Gotron Reference A000066[6]
- Visaton miniature speaker 5cm (2") 1/2W 50 Ohm: Gotron reference K50FL-50[7]
- USB cable V2.0 - USB A to USB B - 1,8m: Gotron reference USBAB-1,8[8]

---

[5]http://www.gotron.be

[6]https://www.gotron.be/arduino-uno-rv3-programmeerbord.html

[7]https://www.gotron.be/licht-geluid/geluid/luidsprekers/mini-luidsprekers/visaton-miniatuur-luidspreker-5cm-2-1-2w-50-ohm.html

[8]https://www.gotron.be/installatie/kabels/computer/usb/usb-kabel-v2-0-usb-a-naar-usb-b-1-8m.html

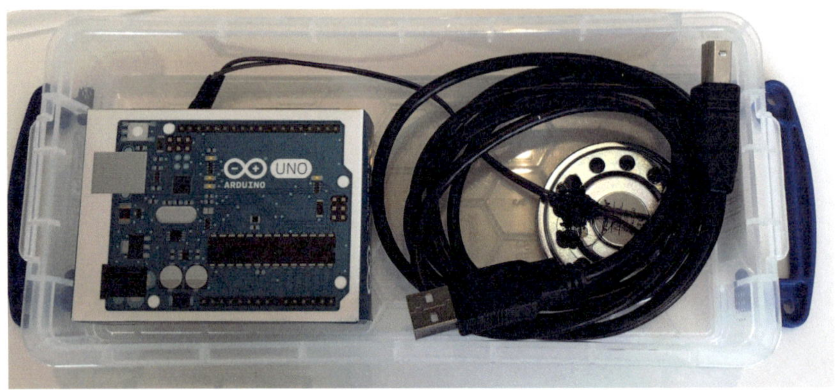

Arduino box

- Set electronic parts for Arduino: Gotron Reference VMA503[9]

---

[9]https://www.gotron.be/set-elektronische-onderdelen-voor-arduino.html

Extra Material box

Library

If you liked the exercises, these books might also be for you.

- Arduino tutorial Open Garage[10], Anthony Liekens
- Arduino for dummies[11], John Nussey
- Arduino project handbook [12], Mark Geddes
- Getting started with Arduino[13], Massimo Banzi
- Arduino Projects for Dummies[14], Brock Craft
- Soldering is easy, here's how to do it![15]
- The computer that was used to go to the moon.[16]

---

[10]http://wiki.opengarage.org/index.php/Arduino_tutorial
[11]https://www.amazon.com/Arduino-Dummies-Computer-Tech/dp/1119489547
[12]https://www.amazon.com/Arduino-Project-Handbook-Practical-Projects-ebook-dp-B01H2KW1QG/dp/B01H2KW1QG
[13]https://www.amazon.com/gp/product/B0027HY20I/
[14]https://www.bol.com/nl/p/arduino-projects-for-dummies/9200000008967085/
[15]https://mightyohm.com/files/soldercomic/FullSolderComic_EN.pdf
[16]https://www.fastcompany.com/90362562/this-computer-changed-world-youve-never-heard-about-it

Helpers

This booklet would not be possible without the help of masses of people.

- Jan Vanwege: Jan is Arduino coach at CoderDojo Gent[17]. He teached me (Geike) Arduino. Jan also helped reviewing this manual.
- My mother Els Ryssen for testing this manual. And asking me questions till she understood it (And I learned to explained it well.)
- My nephew Tijl Gyssels reading the text and gave me tips to make things more understandable.
- At @CoderDojo Gent Leon Wardenaar, Seppe Heyvaert, Seppe Meilander, Wodan De Rave were the first enthusiastic guinea pigs from this workshop. I also processed their feedback.
- Nele Van Beveren gave us some good ideas, including the ingenious idea of explaining comments in comments.
- Laura Dobbelaere gave me a good idea for extensions, and pointed out that I had not yet explained **IF**.
- Laura Dobbelaere, Lize Maton for co-facilitating at CoderDojo4Divas in 2018.

---

[17]http://gent.coderdojoBelgium.be

Geike, Lize, Laura

- Thanks to Emme Dugardyn, it is now clearer that LED lights have two different legs.
- Emme Dugardyn for co-facilitating at Maker Faire Ghent in 2019. (And the advertising we made together on Coolest Project 2019.)
- Thank you Sari 2.0[18] for the changes you send for the Dutch version to my father.

---

[18]https://twitter.com/Sari2_0

Selfie from Geike & Emme at Maker Faire Gent

- Simon from Elektronica voor jou[19] for the tips about Arduino guidelines.
- We used Fritzing[20] for the beautiful drawings of the schemas. If you found these drawings useful, you can support them with some money through their website.

Thank you all..

G

---

[19] www.ElektronicaVoorJou.nl
[20] http://fritzing.org/home/

Versions

As this book is published both as e-book and paperback we will keep track of versions online.
Versions & Errata[21]

- Version 3: Added an errata and version page. Also some changes send by Sari.
- Version 2: Updated all pictures for arduino guidelines. Fixed wrong connection schema in addition 10.
- Version 1: first version

---

[21]https://www.hanoulle.be/book/arduinowithgeike/

Extension one: let the light stay on twice as long.

Assignment:

What should you adjust so that the light stays on twice as long as it stays off.

Code:

Solution extension

```
1   const int ArduinoLightPin = 13;
2   const int TimeOn = 2000;
3   const int TimeOff = 1000;
4
5   void setup() {
6     // We set the pin to the OUTPUT position
7     pinMode(ArduinoLightPin, OUTPUT);
8   }
9
10  void loop() {
11    // We turn the light on
12    digitalWrite(ArduinoLightPin, HIGH);
13    // We wait two seconds
```

```
14    delay(TimeOn);
15    // We turn the light off
16    digitalWrite(ArduinoLightPin, LOW);
17    // We wait a second
18    delay(TimeOff);
19  }
```

Extension two: led light on pin 8

Assignment:

What should you adjust so that the LED blinks when you use pin 8.

Connecting:

We have to move the green jumper wire from pin 9 to pin 8.

Code:

Solution extension

```
1  const int GreenLedLightPin = 8;
2  const int TimeOn = 1000;
3  const int TimeOff = 1000;
4
5  void setup() {
6    // We set the pin to the output position
7    pinMode(GreenLedLightPin, OUTPUT);
8  }
9
10 void loop() {
```

```
11      // We turn the LED light on
12    digitalWrite(GreenLedLightPin,HIGH);
13     // We wait a second
14    delay(TimeOn);
15   // We turn the LED light off
16    digitalWrite(GreenLedLightPin, LOW);
17    // We wait a second
18    delay(TimeOff);
19  }
```

Indeed this expansion is not that difficult. But certainly test them on your Arduino. It is important that you know these steps well. And that they work before we go to the next step.

Extension three: pause between the lights

Assignment:

What should you adjust so that between the two lights, there is a pause of 2.000 milliseconden.

Connecting:

No changes from exercise three.

Code:

Solution extension

```
1   const int GreenLedLightPin = 8;
2   const int ArduinoLightPin = 13;
3
4   int TimeArduino = 10000;
5   int TimeGreen = 1000;
6   int TimeWaiting = 2000;
7
8   void setup() {
9
10    // We set the pins to the output position
```

```
11    pinMode(GreenLedLightPin, OUTPUT);
12    pinMode(ArduinoLightPin, OUTPUT);
13  }
14
15  void loop() {
16     // We turn the Arduino light on and
17     // the green light off.
18     digitalWrite(ArduinoLightPin,HIGH);
19     digitalWrite(GreenLedLightPin, LOW);
20
21     // We wait ten seconds
22     delay(TimeArduino);
23
24     digitalWrite(ArduinoLightPin,LOW);
25     digitalWrite(GreenLedLightPin, LOW);
26
27     // We wait two seconds
28     delay(TimeWaiting);
29
30     // We turn the Arduino light off and
31     // the green light on.
32     digitalWrite(GreenLedLightPin, HIGH);
33
34     // We wait a second
35     delay(TimeGreen);
36  }
```

Here you also notice a lack of clarity in the assignment. Is the break only necessary between the swap from the Arduino light to the green light or also between the green light to the Arduino light?

Did you ask that question (to yourself or the supervisor?)

before you started the assignment? Or have you immediately decided that this or the other is the solution?

That too is programming, properly understanding the question of your "customer".

And taking a decision if she is not available. You might loose too much time if you have to keep waiting for your customer. Take a decision, and be sure to demo your solution to the customer and ask her if it was the right decision. Take into account that you might change your decision in about 20%. That is still way more productive than waiting 100% of the time.

Extension four: remove the waiting time

Assignment:

What should you adjust to ensure that there is no longer any waiting time between the Arduino light and the red LED?

Connecting:

No changes from exercise four.

Code:

Solution extension

```
1   //const int GreenLedLightPin = 8;
2   const int RedLedLightPin = 10;
3   const int ArduinoLightPin = 13;
4
5   const int TimeArduino = 10000;
6   //const int TimeGreen = 1000;
7   cont int TimeRed = 1000;
8
9   void setup() {
10      // We set the pins to the output position
```

```
11    pinMode(RedLedLightPin, OUTPUT);
12    pinMode(ArduinoLightPin, OUTPUT);
13  }
14
15  void loop() {
16    // We turn the Arduino light on and
17    // the red light off.
18    digitalWrite(ArduinoLightPin,HIGH);
19    digitalWrite(RedLedLightPin, LOW);
20
21    // We wait ten seconds
22    delay(TijdArduino);
23
24    // We turn the Arduino light off and
25    // the red light on.
26
27    digitalWrite(ArduinoLightPin,LOW);
28    digitalWrite(RedLedLightPin, HIGH);
29
30    // We wait a second
31    delay(TimeRed);
32  }
```

Be careful, we did not only remove code, we also moved a
line.

Extension five: random time red light

Assignment:

What should you adjust so that the red light stays on for a random time?

Tip: search the internet for the combination of Arduino and random.
Search the internet for the combination of Arduino and random. Or use the reference work that was installed with the Arduino software. Go to the Help menu and then Reference work.

The Reference Work opens with a "glossary". You can click on each word for more explanation. What we are looking for is in the right-hand column at the bottom, under Random Numbers.
If it gives a problem on your computer, you can also find the info on random online[22]

Tip:

There are two functions that we need:

---

[22]https://www.arduino.cc/reference/en/language/functions/random-numbers/random/

- randomSeed(analogRead(0));
- random(min, max);

Computers have a problem of creating random events. That is why we use the first function to make a sort of initialisation of the random function. This way the randomseed gets a number to be really random. We send this function a value that we read from the pin a (This pin is now connected to nothing, and therefore reads a kind of noise. And noise is always random.) The second function gives us a random value that lies between the minimum and maximum that we provide as parameters.

Connecting:

The connection does not change from exercise five.

Code:

Solution extension

```
const int GreenLedLightPin = 8;
const int RedLedLightPin = 10;
//const int ArduinoLightPin = 13;

//const int TimeArduino = 10000;
const int TimeGreen = 10000;
//const int TimeRed = 20000;

const int MinRandom=100;
const int MaxRandom=10000;

```

```cpp
long RandomTime;

void setup() {
  // We set the pins to the output position
  pinMode(RedLedLightPin, OUTPUT);
  pinMode(GreenLedLightPin, OUTPUT);
  randomSeed(analogRead(0));
}

void loop() {
  // We turn the green light on and
  // the red light off.
  digitalWrite(GreenLedLightPin,HIGH);
  digitalWrite(RedLedLightPin, LOW);

  // We wait ten seconds
  delay(TimeGreen);

  // We turn the green light off and
  // the red light on.
  digitalWrite(GreenLedLightPin,LOW);
  digitalWrite(RedLedLightPin, HIGH);

  // We calculate the random time for
  // the red light.
  // This time is between MinRandom and MaxRandom.

  RandomTime = random( MinRandom, MaxRandom);

  delay(RandomTime);
}
```

We use long in this code. Long is a type variable just like int. With an int the value is between -32.768 and 32.767. The value of long is between -2.147,483,648 and 2,147,483,647.
The random function returns a long. (That is why we have to use that type, to make our code work.) As this is a larger number, we also have more randomness.

The random part (line 39 and line 41), are at the end of the loop function. We could also have put these lines between 21 and 22. Then we start with waiting a random time.

This was the hardest extension. If you did not find this immediately, don't curse to hard. I wanted to challenge you.

Extension six: remove random time

Assignment:

In this extension you need to remove the random functionality out the exercise.

Connecting:

The connection does not change

Code:

Solution extension six

```
1   const int GreenLedLightPin = 8;
2   const int YellowLedLightPin = 9;
3   const int RedLedLightPin = 10;
4
5   const int TimeGreen = 10000;
6   const int TimeYellow = 10000;
7   const int TimeRed = 20000;
8
9   void setup() {
10    // We set the pins to the output position
```

```arduino
11    pinMode(RedLedLightPin, OUTPUT);
12    pinMode(YellowLedLightPin, OUTPUT);
13    pinMode(GreenLedLightPin, OUTPUT);
14  }
15
16  void loop() {
17    // We turn the yellow light on and
18    // the red light off.
19    digitalWrite(YellowLedLightPin,HIGH);
20    digitalWrite(RedLedLightPin, LOW);
21
22    // We wait ten seconds
23    delay(TimeYellow);
24
25    // We turn the yellow light off and
26    // the red light on.
27    digitalWrite(YellowLedLightPin,LOW);
28    digitalWrite(RedLedLightPin, HIGH);
29
30    // We wait twenty seconds
31    delay(TimeRed);
32  }
```

Extension seven: blinking yellow light

Assignment:

In this extension, the intention is to make the yellow light blink during the waiting time.

Connecting:

No changes in the connection from exercise seven.

Code:

Solution extension

```
const int GreenLedLightPin = 8;
const int YellowLedLightPin = 9;
const int RedLedLightPin = 10;

const int TimeGreen = 20000;
const int TimeYellow = 1000;
const int TimeRed = 20000;

void setup() {
  // We set the pins to the output position
```

```cpp
11    pinMode(RedLedLightPin, OUTPUT);
12    pinMode(YellowLedLightPin, OUTPUT);
13    pinMode(GreenLedLightPin, OUTPUT);
14  }
15
16  void loop() {
17    // We turn the green light on and
18    // the yellow & red light off.
19    digitalWrite(GreenLedLightPin,HIGH);
20    digitalWrite(YellowLedLightPin, LOW);
21    digitalWrite(RedLedLightPin, LOW);
22
23     // We wait twenty seconds
24    delay(TimeGreen);
25
26    // We turn the yellow light on and
27    // the green & red light off.
28    digitalWrite(GreenLedLightPin, LOW);
29    digitalWrite(YellowLedLightPin, HIGH);
30    digitalWrite(RedLedLightPin, LOW);
31
32    // blink
33    delay(TimeYellow);
34    digitalWrite(YellowLedLightPin, LOW);
35    delay(TimeYellow);
36    digitalWrite(YellowLedLightPin, HIGH);
37    delay(TimeYellow);
38    digitalWrite(YellowLedLightPin, LOW);
39    delay(TimeYellow);
40    digitalWrite(YellowLedLightPin, HIGH);
41    delay(TimeYellow);
42
43    // We turn the red light on and
```

```
44    // the yellow & green light off.
45    digitalWrite(GreenLedLightPin, LOW);
46    digitalWrite(YellowLedLightPin, LOW);
47    digitalWrite(RedLedLightPin, HIGH);
48
49    // We wait twenty seconds
50    delay(TimeRed);
51  }
```

Extension eight: There is no extension eight

Assignment:

Connecting:

Code:

Extension nine: alternating sound

Assignment:

With this expansion you have to alternate the sound between 960 hertz and 770 hertz. The period for a sound must be 1.3 seconds.

Connecting:

No changes in the connection from exercise nine.

Code:

Solution extension

```
1   const int SpeakerPin = 2;
2   const int ButtonPin = 4;
3   const int GreenLedLightPin = 8;
4   const int YellowLedLightPin = 9;
5   const int RedLedLightPin = 10;
6
7   const int TimeGreen = 20000;
8   const int TimeYellow = 1000;
9   const int TimeRed = 10000;
```

```cpp
10   const int TimeSpeaker = 1300;
11
12   //const int  StuttgartPitchFrequency  = 440;
13   const int  HighPitchFrequency  = 960;
14   const int  LowPitchFrequency   = 770;
15
16   int ButtonStatus = 0;
17
18   void setup() {
19    // We set the pins to the output position
20     pinMode(RedLedLightPin, OUTPUT);
21     pinMode(YellowLedLightPin, OUTPUT);
22     pinMode(GreenLedLightPin, OUTPUT);
23     pinMode(ButtonPin, INPUT);
24     pinMode(SpeakerPin, OUTPUT);
25   }
26
27   void loop() {
28     // We turn the green light on and
29     // the yellow & red light off.
30     digitalWrite(GreenLedLightPin,HIGH);
31     digitalWrite(YellowLedLightPin, LOW);
32     digitalWrite(RedLedLightPin, LOW);
33
34     ButtonStatus = digitalRead(ButtonPin);
35
36     if (ButtonStatus == HIGH) {
37
38           // We turn the green light on and
39            // the yellow & red light off.
40             digitalWrite(GreenLedLightPin,HIGH);
41             digitalWrite(YellowLedLightPin, LOW);
42             digitalWrite(RedLedLightPin, LOW);
```

```
43
44          // blink
45          delay(TimeYellow);
46             digitalWrite(YellowLedLightPin, LOW);
47             delay(TimeYellow);
48             digitalWrite(YellowLedLightPin, HIGH);
49             delay(TimeYellow);
50             digitalWrite(YellowLedLightPin, LOW);
51             delay(TimeYellow);
52             digitalWrite(YellowLedLightPin, HIGH);
53             delay(TimeYellow);
54
55          // We turn the red light on and
56             // the yellow & green light off.
57             digitalWrite(GreenLedLightPin, LOW);
58             digitalWrite(YellowLedLightPin, LOW);
59          digitalWrite(RedLedLightPin, HIGH);
60
61          tone(SpeakerPin, HighPitchFrequency, TimeSpeaker)
62           // We wait 1,3 seconds
63            delay(TimeSpeaker);
64          tone(SpeakerPin, LowPitchFrequency, TimeSpeaker)
65           // We wait 1,3 seconds
66            delay(TimeSpeaker);
67          tone(SpeakerPin, HighPitchFrequency, TimeSpeaker)
68           // We wait 1,3 seconds
69            delay(TimeSpeaker);
70          tone(SpeakerPin, LowPitchFrequency, TimeSpeaker)
71           // We wait 1,3 seconds
72            delay(TimeSpeaker);
73          tone(SpeakerPin, HighPitchFrequency, TimeSpeaker)
74           // We wait 1,3 seconds
75            delay(TimeSpeaker);
```

```
76          tone(SpeakerPin, LowPitchFrequency, TimeSpeaker)
77           // We wait 1,3 seconds
78            delay(TimeSpeaker);
79          tone(SpeakerPin, HighPitchFrequency, TimeSpeaker)
80           // We wait 1,3 seconds
81            delay(TimeSpeaker);
82          tone(SpeakerPin, LowPitchFrequency, TimeSpeaker)
83           // We wait 1,3 seconds
84            delay(TimeSpeaker);
85            }
86  }
```

Extension ten: the complete exercise

Assignment:

In this assignment we will add a pedestrian light next to the traffic light.
Think for a moment how a traffic light and a pedestrian light work together.
The pedestrian light consists of a red and green LED.

To help you on your way, we have the connection here.

Connecting:

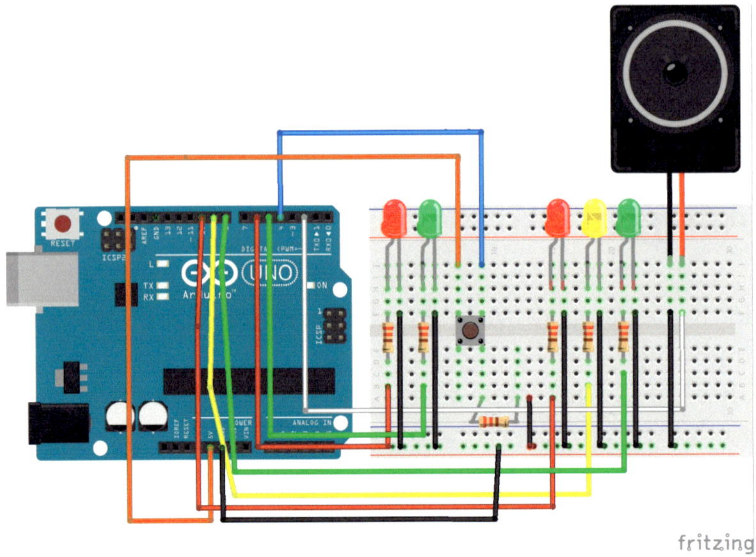

Connection exercise 10

Code:

Oh you thought you would find the code for exercise ten here? Sorry, I think you've learned enough to find it yourself.

Yes, you are now a true Arduino programmer. And real programmers have to think for themselves how they will program something.

Lots of fun.

Geike

Who is Geike

My name is Geike Hanoulle.

I'm born in Ghent (Belgium) on October 12, 2007.
My hobbies are dancing, scouting, reading, programming and giving presentations.

When I was two and a half, my family moved to live half a year in France.
While my brothers went to a French school, I stayed with my mother the whole time.

When I was seven I went to CoderDojo Ghent and learned to program in Scratch.
During my ninth year I learned to program in Arduino.

My first Dutch presentation was at BarCamp Ghent in 2011. Although I only spoke a few sentences, I love doing presentations since that moment.

After going twice to the Dojo4Divas, I was asked if I wanted to facilitate a workshop on the event in October 2018. The book you have been reading was originally created as the Dutch manual for that workshop.

My first English presentation[23] was at AgileIndia in 2019.
The English I spoke I learned from youtube.

---

[23]https://www.youtube.com/watch?v=YAxUwZzlMJE

Translation

This book is translated by Yves Hanoulle.
Yves is not a native English speaker. He has chosen to translate his daughters book himself, to be sure the language of the book, stays the closest possible to the language of his daughter. The goal was not to have perfect English, the goal was to have an English version of his daughters book, as if she had written it herself in English.
If you have a better idea. Feel free to send an e-mail to mailing+translation@hanoulle.be.

Luckily Yves had help from a lot of friends on twitter, when he was looking for other words.

A big thank you to:

- Ben Linders[24]
- Bert Heymans[25]
- Chenling[26]
- Karen Van de Cruys[27]
- Klaas Arduinois[28]
- Kurt Häusler[29]
- Olivier[30]

[24]https://twitter.com/BenLinders
[25]https://twitter.com/bertheymans
[26]https://twitter.com/chenlingzhang
[27]https://twitter.com/karenvdc
[28]https://twitter.com/DonArdonio
[29]https://twitter.com/Kurt_Haeusler
[30]https://twitter.com/inframe

- Michiel Van de Velde[31]
- Rik D'huyvetters[32]
- Rob Roemers[33]
- Robin Malfait[34]
- Zomermaandje[35]

---

[31]https://twitter.com/MieMichiel
[32]https://twitter.com/RikDhuyvetters
[33]https://twitter.com/rroemers
[34]https://twitter.com/malfaitrobin
[35]https://twitter.com/zomermaantje

Made in the USA
Monee, IL
07 July 2026